W9-DEW-860

Norwood and Eloise
Waterhouse:
Starters of Churches

EVELYN VAUGHN
Illustrated by Ron Hester

BROADMAN PRESS
Nashville, Tennessee

To
Norwood and Eloise Waterhouse
who loved churches and left them
to start other churches

© Copyright 1985 • Broadman Press
All rights reserved
4242-94
ISBN: 0-8054-4294-4
Dewey Decimal Classification: J266.092
Subject Headings: WATERHOUSE, NORWOOD / /
WATERHOUSE, ELOISE / / MISSIONS—NEW ENGLAND STATES
Library of Congress Catalog Card Number: 85-6718
Printed in the United States of America

Library of Congress Cataloging in Publication Data

Vaughn, Evelyn, 1923–
Norwood and Eloise Waterhouse.

(Meet the missionary)
Summary: A biography of the missionary couple with
emphasis on their mission work in New England.
1. Waterhouse, Norwood—Juvenile literature.
2. Waterhouse, Eloise—Juvenile literature.
3. Missions, Home—Juvenile literature. 4. Missions—
New England—Juvenile literature. 5. Missionaries—New
England—Biography—Juvenile literature. [1. Waterhouse,
Norwood. 2. Norwood, Eloise. 3. Missionaries]
I. Hester, Ronald, ill. II. Title. III. Series.

BV2765.5.A1V38   1985 266'.6132'0922 [B] [920] 85-6718
ISBN 0-8054-4294-4

Contents

Revival in a Barn

"Yes, you may sit with your friends. But you will have to be quiet," Norwood's mother said.

Norwood lived in South Carolina. He liked to go to church. He liked to listen to the sermon. He was glad he was old enough to sit with his friends.

"Jesus loves every person," the preacher said one Sunday. "Jesus wants you to trust him. He wants to be your Savior."

The sermon was over. Norwood went to talk to the preacher.

"I told Jesus that I loved him," Norwood said. "I want to do what he wants me to do."

The preacher talked to Norwood. They both talked with Norwood's parents.

"I asked Jesus to forgive my sins," Norwood said. "I asked him to be my Savior."

"We are very happy, Norwood," his parents said.

At the next worship service, Norwood joined the church. He was not very tall. He stood in a chair to shake hands with people.

"God bless you," the church members said.

"We will pray for you. We are very happy."

The next day Norwood went to school. His mind was not on his school work. He thought about trusting Jesus as his Savior.

When school was over, Norwood ran home. "Mama, I wish I could tell everybody in the world what happened to me." And he did tell his friends.

When Norwood was thirteen, a famous preacher came to town. His name was Gipsy Smith. He came to preach a revival. The revival services were held in an old barn.

Quietly, Norwood listened to Gipsy Smith preach. Norwood felt that God wanted him to do something special.

"Show me what to do, Lord," Norwood said. "I will do it."

Several years later, Norwood's father was hurt in a car accident. "Father needs my help in his business. I will help him sell stationery. I will try to be a good salesman. But, most of all, I want to serve you, Lord," Norwood prayed.

Something Different

About this same time, a young girl was growing up in Georgia. Her name was Eloise Rodgers. Once she said, "I will never be a preacher's wife." But that was when she was eight years old.

Now Eloise was a young woman. She lived in Florida. She worked in a college cafeteria.

"I like being a dietitian," she told a friend. "I like working in this college. But I don't want to work here always. I want to do something different with my life."

Eloise traveled from Georgia to Florida on a bus. On one trip, she met Norwood Waterhouse.

They became friends. They wrote many letters. They got to know each other through their letters. They also came to love each other.

"I am thinking of becoming a preacher," Norwood wrote in one of his letters.

"I would like to work with Norwood," Eloise thought. "Together we could do more for God than either of us could do alone."

One day Eloise was talking to a friend. "I'd like to talk to your pastor."

"About what?" her friend asked.

9

"About becoming a Baptist," Eloise said.

"But you're a Methodist," the friend said. "Do you really want to be a Baptist?"

"Norwood has asked me to marry him," Eloise said. "We have been talking about beliefs. I really do believe like Baptists do. And if I am going to be the wife of a Baptist preacher, I should be a Baptist."

Not long after that, Eloise did become a Baptist. Later, on July 5, 1946, Eloise and Norwood were married.

Children We Love

Eloise and Norwood had moved to Kentucky. Their first child was born there. They named him Woody.

When Woody was ten years old, he had a big surprise.

"Happy birthday, Woody. Your mother has a surprise for you. A special birthday cake," his dad said.

"Wow! what a cake!" Woody could hardly believe what he saw. His mother knew his favorite food was hamburgers. She had made him the biggest hamburger he had ever seen. The bun was twelve inches across. On top was one candle for age ten. "I will never forget this birthday cake," Woody laughed.

The second child born to Eloise and Norwood was Deborah. They lived in Indiana when she was born.

Deborah loved to travel. "I want to go camping," five-year-old Deborah said one day.

"No, this trip is for the boys in the church," said her dad.

"I want to go. I'll be a good camper," Deborah said.

Norwood went to the church. There he met the boys. They were ready for the camping trip. He told them how much Deborah wanted to go camping.

"Let her go with us," they all said.

Norwood called his wife on the telephone.
"Get Deborah ready to go camping," he said.
"We will come by and get her."

Norwood and the boys drove to the house.
Deborah was sitting on the steps. She was ready
to go. As she had promised, she was one of the
best campers.

Lisa, the third Waterhouse child was born in
Connecticut. She like to climb. She was known
as a climber.

"Where is Lisa?" asked her mother.

No one knew.

"I'll look for her. She can't be far away," her dad said. He walked down the street. Soon he could hear five-year-old Lisa calling.

"Help, Daddy! Get me down," she begged. Lisa was stuck in a tree. She had climbed up the tree. But she couldn't get down.

"Jump, Lisa." Her daddy stood under the tree. He held out his arms. Lisa jumped. She knew her daddy would catch her.

Norwood Waterhouse held Lisa in his arms. "Children are a joy and a blessing from God," he thought.

A Special Church

Norwood and Eloise Waterhouse worked in many churches. They helped start churches in different states. Some of the time they helped churches in Georgia, Kentucky, Indiana, and South Carolina. Some of the time they worked with churches in Nebraska, Connecticut, and Vermont. Each church in each state was special.

One special church in Connecticut was a Slavic church. Several languages were spoken in that church. Sometimes most of the people spoke Russian. Bibles printed in Russian were used. The sermon was preached in Russian. Songs were sung in Russian.

At other times the sermon was in other languages. Bibles and songs were in those languages. When most of the people in the church spoke a certain language, that language was used.

One night the church had a special worship service. A group of Russian people were there. They came from a home for older people.

One lady in the group was deaf. She could not hear. She could not talk. But she wanted to be with her Christian friends.

15

Elias Golonka was in the worship service that night. He could speak the Russian language. Rodney Webb was there also. He was a missionary to the deaf.

The preacher preached in Russian. Elias Golonka whispered the words in English to Rodney Webb. Rodney used sign language to tell or show the sermon with his hands.

The woman who could not hear, smiled. She could not hear the words, but she could see the sermon in sign language.

A Man Named Friday

Friday was a college student. He was over six feet tall. He weighed about 275 pounds. He had long hair. His clothes were strange looking.

During the 1960s some young people were called "hippies." The way they dressed was different from other young people. The way they acted was often different, too. Friday was one of these young people.

The East Hartford church in Connecticut cared about all kinds of people. They cared about young people like Friday. Norwood Waterhouse helped church members think about the people where they lived. He helped them think especially about the people who did not go to church.

"We could start some mission churches," Norwood said. "More people could learn about God. More people would have a place to worship."

The East Hartford church met in a house. It started six mission churches. They did not have church buildings of their own. One of them met in a home. One met in a school. Another met in a motel. Others met in other places.

The church members started a coffeehouse. Coffee and other refreshments were served there. It was a favorite place for young people to come. They sang and talked with one another. It was a place where Christian young people told others about Jesus.

Many times hippies like Friday came to the coffeehouse. Young people at the coffeehouse invited the hippies to the church services.

One Sunday night, Friday went to the church service. He sat on the front row. After the sermon, Norwood Waterhouse baptized some new

Christians. He talked about the meaning of baptism.

"Baptism," he said, "is a way of saying that I am already a Christian. Now, I want to try to live like one."

Friday jumped to his feet. "That's for me," he said. "I want to follow Christ. I am a Christian. I want to be baptized."

Friday was a happy Christian. He told other hippies about Jesus. Many of them became Christians, too.

Sugar House

"Come to our house. You are all invited," said Norwood Waterhouse.

"Let's go," the church members said. "We will have a good time."

The Waterhouses lived in Vermont now. They often had guests in their home. They liked having church members in their home.

Sometimes the church members had overnight retreats. They sang and had Bible study. They played games and ate together.

One time the Waterhouses planned a trip to a sugar house.

"Is this the day?" Sara asked. Sara was one of the children in the church. "Are we going to a sugar house?"

"Yes," said Mrs. Waterhouse. "You will see how Vermont's famous maple syrup is made."

The children were excited. They liked to watch the syrup-makers.

Soon they were at the sugar house. Steam came out the openings in the roof of the sugar house. Inside, the syrup-maker was busy stirring the boiling sap (juice) from maple trees.

"What is he doing?" Sara asked.

"He is cooking the sap to make syrup," Mr. Waterhouse told her.

"How did he catch the sap when it ran out of the trees?" Sara asked.

"The syrup-maker hung buckets on the maple trees," Mr. Waterhouse told her. "The sap ran out of the trees through a little faucet. It ran into the buckets. The syrup-maker had a big tank on a sled. The sled is pulled by a tractor. It may be pulled by horses. The syrup-maker poured the sap out of the buckets into the tank. Then he

brought the sap to the sugar house. Sometimes it is called a syrup house."

Sara watched the syrup-maker. He poured some sap into a pot and cooked it on a gas camp stove. The rest of the sap cooked in the big vat.

"Why is he cooking some of the sap longer in the pot?" Sara asked.

"You will see," her pastor said. "The syrup-maker is making a special treat for us."

Some of the boys brought in buckets of snow. Each person was given snow in a small bowl. From the pot, the syrup-maker poured a spoonful of thick syrup on the snow. It was like candy.

"Oh, this is good. I like it," said Sara.

"People in Vermont call it 'sugar on snow,'" said Mrs. Waterhouse.

"I like sugar on snow," said Sara. I like being in Vermont. I like being in this church. I like the things we do together."

Beloved Home

"What a big garage," said Norwood. "Just think what we can do with it."

The garage was a gift. It was a gift from the church in Connecticut. Norwood and Eloise were ready to retire. They were moving to Vermont.

"The garage will make a lovely chalet," said Eloise. (A chalet is a type of house used in the mountains in Switzerland.) "How can we move it to Vermont?"

"We'll cut it into many parts," Norwood told her. "We can haul the parts in a truck."

Finally, Norwood and Eloise were ready to move. Up, up they drove. They drove high into the mountains. Like a turtle, they took their home with them. Soon all of the parts were moved. The house that started in Connecticut was now in Vermont. But the house was in many pieces.

Norwood and Eloise began putting the parts of the garage back together. They worked for a long time. Their house has plenty of room. It now has an attic and a porch. It also has a fireplace.

The Waterhouses like to look out the large windows in their house. Every season is different. The mountains are covered with wild flowers in the spring and fall. In the winter the snow is deep. Then the fireplace makes the house warm and cozy. In the summer the breezes from the mountains are cool.

"This is a wonderful home," Eloise and Norwood told a friend. "We should give it a special name. You speak German. We would like for our chalet to have a German name."

"I agree," said their friend. "I know a good name for your chalet. Call it *Lieberheim* (LEE ber hime). *Lieberheim* is a German word. It means 'beloved home' or 'the home we love.'"

An Exciting Future

"'Retire' means to leave something. 'Retire' means to stop what you have been doing," said Norwood. "Eloise and I can't really leave the work we love. And we don't want to stop doing what we love to do. For years we have started new churches. We still want to do that here in Vermont."

"We have more time now," said Eloise. "Yet, we are always busy. We read. We study a lot. We work with churches. Norwood prepares sermons. I teach a Sunday School class. We both work in Vacation Bible School."

"Being retired gives time for extras," said Norwood. "Eloise and I enjoy our hobbies. I like oil painting. She arranges flowers."

"I like to arrange flowers for the church," Eloise said. "I also teach women in the church how to arrange flowers."

"For Christmas we gave each other cross-country skis. We are still learning to use them," Eloise laughed. "We also have snowshoes.

We love to walk through the woods in the snow."

"Life is exciting at any age," said Norwood.

"I know the future will be good," added
Eloise. "God is leading us. We believe he has
more for us to do."

"God has supplied our needs in more ways than we can say," said Norwood. "We know that Philippians 4:19 is true. For years Eloise and I have had an agreement with God. Our promise and his are in the Bible. They can be found in Proverbs 3:5-6.

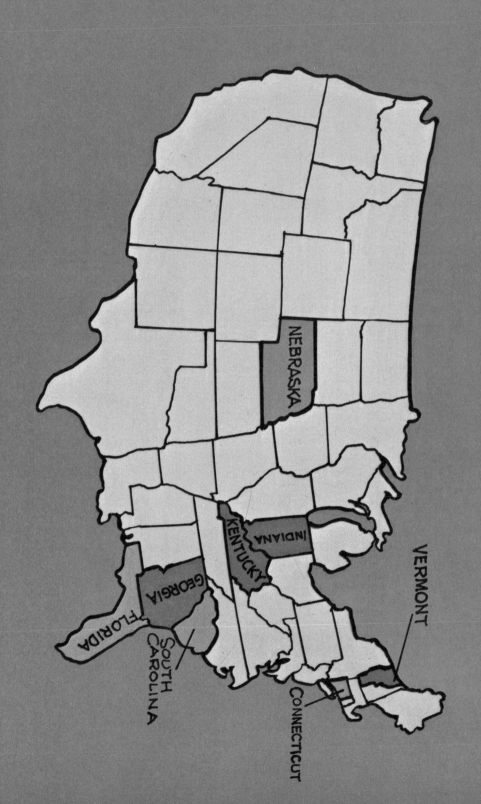

Remember

Norwood and Eloise Waterhouse knew that God had a good plan for their lives.

Where was Norwood when he felt that God wanted him to do something special? What did Norwood say to God?

Why was Eloise not satisfied in her work as a dietitian? What did she want to do with her life?

The Waterhouses loved their own family and their church members. Sometimes they called church members their church families. How did the Waterhouses show love to their children? What are some things the Waterhouses did for people in their church families and for others? What are some ways you can show love to other people?

Look at the map. In how many states did Norwood and Eloise live and work? Where would you like to live and work when you grow up?

About the Author

Evelyn Vaughn lives in Jackson, Mississippi. Evelyn's husband is named Chester. They have two children. Their names are Jim and Harriet.

Evelyn teaches children in the First Baptist Church, Jackson, Mississippi. She also writes materials for children and their teachers at church.

Before she wrote this book, Evelyn visited Norwood and Eloise Waterhouse in Vermont. She talked to them about their lives and work. She says, "Getting to know the Waterhouses was a special joy."

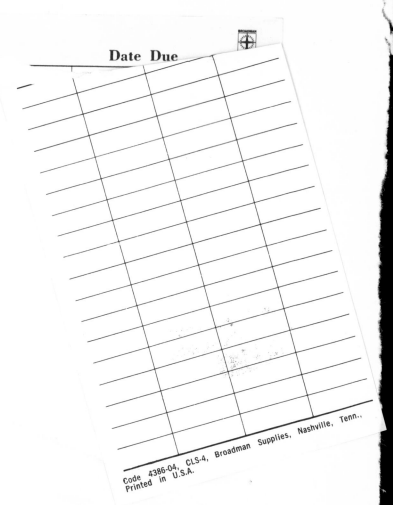

Date Due

Code 4386-04, CLS-4, Broadman Supplies, Nashville, Tenn.,
Printed in U.S.A.